You're My Dawg, Dog

A LEXICON OF
DOG TERMS FOR PEOPLE

You're My Dawg, Dog

A LEXICON OF
DOG TERMS FOR PEOPLE

By Donald Friedman
Illustrations by J.C. Suarès

welcome
BOOKS

For the loyal companions:
Puck Friedman, Marley Palmer, Stella Pusateri,
Buddy Shapiro, (Harry) Bing Stiles,
and the late Linda Lukens, Brubeck Brodzinsky,
Babe Schwartz, Indiana Jones Harris,
Casey Leopold, Deke Lowenstein, Harry Isler,
Bart (Bartholomew James) Nora,
Clapton Palmer, and their loving masters.

Outside of a dog,

a book is man's best friend.

Inside of a dog, it's too dark to read.

GROUCHO MARX

Dog (n) (*Canis lupus familiaris*) The wolf that after 30,000 years of domestication became the hairless xolo that shocked Columbus, a poodle you can stick in your pocket, and a border collie with a thousand-word vocabulary. Most especially, man's best friend, his protector, helper, companion. Today, the dog detects cancers, seizures, and blood sugar levels, not to mention bombs, drugs, and missing people. He guards your home, hunts, herds, draws sleds and carts, soldiers, and carries messages. He leads you when you're blind, gives you signals when you're deaf, tows your wheelchair when you're disabled. He regulates your heart. Your dog is the ultimate acolyte; he believes you are the very image of God. His centrality to our lives has led inevitably to an equally central place in our language—the word "dog" alone or as part of a description of dog qualities or behaviors finds dozens of everyday applications.

"The Great Catrine turned out to be a real *dog.*"

2. The person in your life who possesses the best of the canine's traits. Your main man. The one who's always got your back. The friend who'll help you bury the body. Also, colloquially, "dawg." "You're my dawg, Josiah." **3.** An auto-antonym, "dog" means, as well, someone who possesses the worst of the canine's traits, someone who exhibits mean, reproachful, or contemptible behavior. "Herb's a real dog for selling knockoff watches to his friends as the real thing." Shylock rebuffs the loan-seeking Antonio with "You spurn'd me such a day; another time / You called me dog." The negative outlook defined by "cynic" finds its origin in the Greek philosophers who were called "Cynics" or "dog-like" ("*kynikos*" in Greek) for their rejection of social conventions.
4. A very unattractive woman. "Sally's decision to shave her head, insert a bone through her nose, and tattoo 'Black Sabbath' on her forehead has turned her into a dog that even dogs shy away from."
5. Something that's failed or performing poorly, like a stock or a Broadway show. "Amalgamated Schmaltz has been the worst dog in the NASDAQ, falling in three months from $75 to 11 cents a share."
6. An iron support for holding fireplace logs. An andiron. Also called a firedog. **7.** One of a large variety of mechanical devices with teeth or claws used for gripping and holding—such as the tool barbers once used for pulling teeth. **8.** (v) To follow closely. "Josiah's beagle used to dog his every step, and since he died Josiah says the memory of his little companion dogs his every waking hour."

Big dog (n) The boss, an important personage, or the most competitive in a field. **2.** The constellation Canis Major. **3.** The Boston Dynamics Big Dog robot, which looks and sounds like a giant mutated insect, can carry several hundred pounds for hours over any kind of terrain without losing its balance even when violently kicked from the side or traversing black ice, and without complaint. See it on YouTube.

Bird dog (n) Like a dog that is trained to find
and retrieve birds, a person whose job is to find
business opportunities. Pejoratively, the guy
who goes after another guy's girl—as in the
Everly Brothers song of the same name with the
admonitory chorus, "Hey bird dog, get away from
my quail / Hey bird dog, you're on the wrong trail."
2. (v) To engage in such practices.

Black dog depression (n) The phrase seems to
conjoin a dark mood with being dogged or
unshakably followed. Commonly associated with
Winston Churchill, who often referred to the
depressive side of his bipolar disorder as his "black
dog." The usage has been around for centuries: in
the Middle Ages, melancholia was one of the less
positive traits the dog represented. "When Sally
told Josiah she couldn't face the day, that she'd
gotten up with a black dog in her bed, he asked
whether it was better or worse than his daily
awakening with an elephant's foot on his chest."

Blue dog (n) A member of the coalition of conservative and some moderate Democratic leaders, which was founded following the 1994 midterm losses by congressional Democrats. Derived from "yellow dog Democrat," its coinage is credited to Pete Geren, a Texas congressman who claimed they'd been "choked blue" by more left-wing Democrats.

Cut dog (n) One that's been neutered. Metaphorically, a man who's been rendered powerless or situationally impotent. Lyndon B. Johnson, marginalized as J.F.K.'s vice president, complained he was "a cut dog."

Dirty dog (n) A pejorative term for someone who is sneaky and underhanded. **2.** A playfully ironic description of someone's craftiness. "I can't believe you pulled it off, you dirty dog!" Similar humorous usages with other adjectives are "sly dog" and "lucky dog."

Dish dog (n) A dishwasher. Analogous constructions: "bar dog" for a bartender, "grill dog" for a short order cook, "ball dog" for a tennis helper, and "bag dog" for a golf caddy. (I just made the last three up—try your own.)

Dog biscuit (n) Fido's motivators became the unflavored crackers issued to British soldiers in World War I as field rations. **2.** An army mattress. The military apparently has a tradition of disparagement with dog prefixes, as in "dog fat" for butter, and the "dogleg medal" awarded for good conduct. And see "dogface," "dog tags," and the Royal Navy's "dogsbody."

Dog box (n) A train carriage without a corridor, each compartment having its own door to the platform.

Dogcart (n) A two-wheeled open cart drawn by a horse.

Dog clutch (n) A disconnectable coupling.

Dog collar (n) A stiff upright collar, especially the reverse collar worn by a clergyman. "Herb could not come to grips with his unfrocking, and for a year afterward continued to wear his dog collar and bask in the deference it inspired in the people he met."

Dog collar

Dog days (n) For the Greeks, the rising of Sirius, the dog star, signaled the start of the hot days of summer, which became known as the dog days. The Greeks offered sacrifices to Sirius to cajole cool breezes. The Romans called the sweltering days "*dies caniculares.*" The French call the scorching August weather "*la canicule.*" This idea—as well as "every dog has its day"—is alluded to in the title of the Sidney Lumet film *Dog Day Afternoon*, starring Al Pacino. "Dog days" has also found new meaning among stock traders who've found August slow for stocks as well as people.

Dog-eared (adj) Turned down or bent over, especially the corners of pages. "Sally gave Herb her copy of *Ulysses* and, given that he'd never seen her read anything more challenging than *Cosmo*, he was dumbstruck when he opened it and found it dog-eared, underlined, and filled with her marginalia." **2.** Worn out, shabby from overuse. "We've been listening to the same dog-eared rhetoric from the same dog-eared senator for forty years now."

Dog-eat-dog (adj) Ruthlessly, brutally competitive. "Advertising is a dog-eat-dog business. But, then, it's hard to find one that isn't." From mishearing, the phrase has found currency as the mangled, meaningless "it's a doggie dog world."

Dog end (n) A cigarette butt.

Dog-eyed (adj) Presenting a sad, begging aspect. "We are unhappy, mild, dog-eyed gentlemen..." is how *Lolita*'s narrator, Humbert Humbert, describes himself and his nymphet-loving peers.

Dogface (n) A U.S. army infantryman, especially in World War II. The term first achieved currency when used by Bill Mauldin, the legendary combat cartoonist, and then by Audie Murphy, the most decorated soldier of the war, in his autobiography *To Hell and Back* and in the 1955 movie with the same title. A song from that movie, "The Dogface Soldier," sold over 300,000 copies and was adopted by the 3rd Infantry Division. The word's origin is unknown but is likely an expression of disgruntlement by soldiers who felt ordered about like dogs, who wore "dog tags," slept in "pup tents," and otherwise lived a "dog's life." **2.** A widespread species of saltwater puffer fish. **3.** The difficult-to-catch butterfly that is California's state insect.

Dog-eyed

Dog-faced liar (n) A compulsive dissembler. Someone who tells blatant lies repeatedly. Mark Twain popularized the earlier coined ascending order of falsehoods: "lies, damn lies, and statistics," but what statistician could hold a candle to our politicians, or our political spinmeisters?

Dog-fall (n) A tie or draw, especially in wrestling when opponents hit the mat simultaneously so that no points are awarded to either. Any contest with no victor.

Dogfight (n) A no-holds-barred brawl. "When Herb found Josiah with his fiancée Sally at the party, it turned into a scene out of *Amores Perros*—the two of them on the floor, Herb biting Josiah's ear like he was Mike Tyson." **2.** One-on-one aerial combat. Two famous dogfighting aces from World War I were Eddie Rickenbacker and Baron Manfred von Richthofen. Battles with the latter were famously parodied by Charles Schulz with the legendary Snoopy fighting from the roof of his Sopwith Camel doghouse.

Dogfight

Dogfish (n) (*squalus acanthias*) The most common of the sharks, they're three to four feet long, travel in schools, and got their nickname from their practice of hunting in packs. They, in turn, are hunted by humans who use them for their skins, for laboratory study, for human and pet food, for liver oil, and for fertilizer. If humans leave them alone, they can live to a hundred.

Dogged (adj) Sullen, obstinate, determined, or obstinately persistent. "Herb and Sally got married only because of Herb's dogged pursuit after she'd rejected him as unfaithful."

Doggerel (n) The origin's unclear, and certainly
not part of the canon, but I'll give it a shot while
you have a beer: "doggerel" is bottom-drawer,
humorous poetry with weak rhymes and little
attention to meter. The word apparently made its
first appearance in *The Canterbury Tales* in 1386 and
has been in continual use since. Because appending
"dog" to another word has been a traditional way of
disparaging the idea expressed—see "dog Latin,"
"dog's life," "dog meat," "dog's breath," etc.—it's
likely that "dog" was being used similarly here, to
suggest a diminished kind of verse.

Doggie bag (n) A container for leftover restaurant food, requested by the patron on the understood pretext that it is for the dog. "I'd like a doggie bag for the asparagus, the eggplant, and the chocolate mousse—Bowser's favorites."

Doggie Day (n) New Year's in the United Kingdom. The day that dog licenses are renewable.

Doggie style (adj) (*Coitus more ferarum*) Not *Vogue* for Airedales and Cocker Spaniels, but copulating in the manner of our canine friends. The Kama Sutra calls it the "congress of the cow," which if nothing else tells you it's been around for a very long time.

Doggo (adv) To be still and quiet (lying like a dog) in concealment. "Herb and Sally, nearly caught *in flagrante delicto*, lay doggo in the thick foliage until the other guests had passed by."

Dog-hearted (adj) Heartless or cruel. Kent observes Lear's unkind folly of stripping Cordelia of her inheritance in favor of her witch-like sisters as giving "her dear rights / To his dog-hearted daughters." To anyone who knows dogs, an obvious misnomer.

Dog hole (n) A low, mean, unsuitable habitation. A dwelling appropriate only for a dog. Clearly the invention of someone unaware of how pets are treated in modern English-speaking countries.

Dog in a doublet (n) Someone of courage and daring. From the practice of dressing boar-hunting dogs in leather doublets.

Dog it (v) To underperform or inadequately exert oneself at work or other tasks. "The coach caught Josiah dogging it on his last three laps around the field, so he made him stay after practice and do ten more."

Dog Latin (n) Barbarously incorrect or ungrammatical Latin, the quintessential example being the familiar "*Illegitimi non carborundum*," which is supposed to mean "Don't let the bastards wear you down" but consists of the wrongly used Latin "*illegitimus*" and the non-existent words "*non*" and "*carborundum*." The late humorist Jean Shepherd created the nonsensical, pretend aphorism "*In hoc agricula conc, in est spittle laud*," which he translated variously, depending on mood and context. In the same sense of spurious or bastardized, we have "dog English," "dog rime," and "dog logic."

Dogleg hole (n) A golf hole whose fairway makes a bend either to the right or the left, usually about 200 yards from the tee, obscuring the green and confronting the player with the decision to either play it safe or try for the carry like one of the "big dogs."

Dogleg stairs (n) A flight of stairs between two floors of a building comprised of two or more straight sections connected by a landing or landings. This makes for a more compact staircase and for privacy on the upper floor.

Dog meat (adj) A pejorative description of human food, implying that it is meat or food fit only for a dog. "Waiter, summon the maître d'—this sirloin is dog meat!" **2.** A description of one's condition after being badly beaten or seriously injured. "Unable to keep his guard up, by the twelfth round Rocky's face was dog meat." **3.** (n) The unthinkable (but sadly real) use of dog flesh as a comestible.

Dog nap (n) Differs from a catnap only in that it's taken sitting up. "When the airlines turned into flying subways, I found it impossible to get any sleep—the best I can hope for is a dog nap."

Dog nobbler (n) A bright fly-fishing lure.

Dog-paddle (n) A swimming stroke in which the swimmer lies on her stomach, head out of the water, and moves her hands forward and back while her legs jerk up and down—going through the water as a dog would. **2.** (v) To swim using the dog-paddle. "While Sally lay indolently on the float, Herb brought her cold drinks and snacks, dog-paddling out to her, pushing the plastic foam tray with his nose."

Dog pile (n) A group of people jumping on top of someone who's fallen, especially in a game. "Josiah was tackled at the ten-yard line, and in seconds there was a dog pile with every nearby player from the other team diving on, until you couldn't help but imagine Josiah flattened on the bottom like a cartoon character under a steamroller." **2.** A quick series of unfriendly responses to an online posting. "Within minutes of Sarah Palin's proposal that any immigrant without a Green Card be jailed and deported without a hearing, there was a dog pile of objections." **3.** The name of a popular metasearch engine that collects and presents the results of other search engines.

Dog rose or **dog briar** (n) (*Rosa canina*) A climbing perennial plant that grows to ten feet or more and whose Vitamin C-rich dried fruit, known as rosehip, has been widely used for years as a folk remedy for colds, fevers, digestive disorders, rheumatism, gout, and other ailments, including, centuries ago, rabies—which is a possible source for its name. It may also have been a way of disparaging the wild shrub by comparison to its cultivated relatives. Dog rose is offered as merely representative of the many canine terms appropriated for botanical purposes—"dog grass" (*triticum caninum*) and "dog cabbage" are two others—which were collected and classified by Tom Burns Haber of Ohio State University in an article entitled "Canine Terms in Popular Names

Dog rose

of Plants." Other names in Haber's list incorporate not only "dog," but also "bitch," "hound," "pup," and "puppy."

Dog salmon (n) Also known as "chum salmon," it's native to the North Pacific and the lowest grade of commercial salmon.

Dogsbody (n) Someone who performs drudge labor. From British Royal Navy slang—first for dried boiled peas that the sailors had to eat, then for the junior officers assigned jobs that senior officers wouldn't do. "Sally kept Herb around as her personal dogsbody, making him chop wood, clean the hen house, muck the stalls, and weed the garden."

Dog shelf (n) The floor, in sarcastic usage. "'Hang it on the dog shelf, Herb!' Sally yelled to him, indicating that he should throw his coat on the floor, as was his habit."

Dog star (n) Sirius, the brightest star in the firmament, owing to its luminosity and proximity

to Earth. So called because of its prominence in the constellation Canis Major (Big Dog), which was also seen as Orion's dog. To the ancient Egyptians, its rising marked the flooding of the Nile and the onset of the hot months. (See "dog days.")

Dog tags (n) Metal identification tags worn by dogs and by members of the military. Dogs wear them attached to their collars, members of the military wear them from chains around their neck. **2.** Fashionable accessories worn by civilians in the style of military dog tags made in a variety of metals, including stainless steel, sterling silver, and gold plate, and engraved with personalized text. "Herb gave Sally a set of gold, emerald-encrusted dog tags, with lyrics of their song, Rihanna's 'Stupid in Love,' inscribed."

Dog-tired (adj) Exhausted. Probably from observing dogs collapsing after long runs, but a more imaginative version of its origin is found in a supposed practice of Alfred the Great, sainted defender of Anglo-Saxon kingdoms against the Vikings. Alfred, the story goes, would make his sons, Athelbrod and Edwin, chase his hunting dogs, and whoever of the dog-tired pair caught more would secure the place of honor at the dinner table. "Dog" is used as an intensifier meaning extremely or thoroughly with other adjectives as well, such as "dog-hungry," "dog-lean," and "dog-poor."

Dogtooth (n) A checked textile pattern with notched corners that is supposed to be larger than the (similarly canine) houndstooth pattern—but who can really tell the difference?

Dogtown (n) A disparaging term for a small town. **2.** A 1997 film about such a place. **3.** A nickname for the Best Friends Animal Sanctuary in Utah.

Dog watch (n) A short watch at sea, usually 4–6p.m. and 6–8p.m., half the length of the normal period, so named presumably because sailors associated it with interrupted "dog sleep" or the brief "dog nap."

Dog whipper (n) Until the 19th century and for several centuries prior, a church official with the responsibility of removing unruly dogs from services. In some venues they were employed to deal with stray dogs anywhere in the village and, therefore, served as early dogcatchers.

Dog-whistle politics (n) From the inaudibility of a dog whistle to humans, the practice of using coded language so that the message is concealed from all but its intended audience—especially to communicate racist or religious sentiments in a veiled way. "States rights" became understood as code for racial segregation. George W. Bush used frequent biblical phrases in his speeches to express his alliance with the aims of the religious right. Of course, given American religious illiteracy, it is likely that the references had no meaning to his hearers other than as code.

Dog with two tails (n) Someone who is very pleased at a particular occurrence. "When Herb got seventh-row seats for *Cats*, Sally was as happy as a dog with two tails."

Dog years (adv) A long time. That said, the seven-to-one ratio that is popularly used to calculate how old a dog would be in human years is not accurate at all. The first year of a dog's life is the equivalent of about ten to fifteen years of a human's—the variations dependent on breed and size. On average, one could use twenty-five human years for the first two dog years and four human years for each of the years that follow.

Dogs (n) Feet, especially feet that ache. "After not finding a cab and being forced to walk fifty blocks in four-inch pumps, Sally's dogs were really barking."

Dog's breakfast (n) A complete mess. Saying President Obama inherited a dog's breakfast from President Bush would be an example of the phrase employed as understatement.

Dog's breath (n) Abusive slang for the halitosis suffered by some people, implying, of course, that dogs' exhalations are malodorous.

Dog's chance (adv) To have little or no chance. "Sally told Herb that, after he forgot the two-month anniversary of the night they met, she felt their relationship had a dog's chance of succeeding."

Dog's dinner (n) Dressed or displayed in a smart and ostentatious fashion. "Herb knew he was in trouble when he showed up in jeans and a t-shirt and Sally opened the door dolled up like a dog's dinner." In no way to be confused with a "dog's breakfast."

Dog's life (n) A wretched existence. "Working in a coal mine is a dog's life."

Dogs of war (n) The soldiery, also mercenaries. "Cry 'Havoc!' and let slip the dogs of war" was Mark Antony's imagined call from the grave for revenge by the murdered Caesar in Shakespeare's *Julius Caesar*. The words urge the army be unleashed like dogs, and (with the order 'Havoc!') allowed to plunder after victory. "Dogs of war" has found widespread usage as book, movie, and song titles, and as the name of computer games. Of course, it also refers more literally to the courageous dogs who have been employed since ancient times to serve in wars as soldiers, scouts, sentries, trackers, and couriers.

Downward-facing dog (n) A widely recognized yoga posture with hands and feet on the floor and tailbone in the air, resembling a dog stretching itself. A rejuvenating stretch for both species.

Hangdog (adj) Dejected, downcast, furtive, or guilty—the expression found on a dog or human when he's just been caught doing something he shouldn't or he's been told he's not going with you. **2.** (n) One who is furtive or sneaky.

Horn dog (n) Someone who thinks about sex all the time and may, as a consequence, become a "tough dog to keep on the porch."

Hot dog (n) A precooked sausage, a frankfurter or weiner, usually served on a bun and *de rigueur* cuisine at a baseball game. From the early accusation that dog was the primary constituent of the emulsified meat that is stuffed in the casing. **2.** (adj) Someone who performs daredevil stunts or shows off. "Herb, ever the hot dog at chess, loved to offer his queen in sacrifice." Sometimes used pejoratively to describe a self-aggrandizing or non-team player. **3.** An exclamation of pleasure; also "hot diggity dog!" With the exception of Pat Boone and maybe Sarah Palin, last known public use was in 1958.

Hot dog

Lapdog (n) Not only the Maltese, Pug, or Pomeranian that can be held on your lap, but someone servile and dependent, happy to do the bidding of another. Prime Minister Tony Blair was regularly accused of being President Bush's lapdog.

Lead dog (n) The musher's treasured Husky or Malamute that heads the sled-pulling team, and, by extension, a person who leads a group within a larger organization.

Lucky dog (n) A very fortunate person, sometimes used to imply undeservedly so. "Herb, that lucky dog, won the lottery the same week his company Amalgamated Schmaltz was awarded a no-bid, cost-plus military supply contract for Iraq, and Paramount gave him a million dollars for the rights to his story."

Lucky dog

Mad dog (n) Someone who is unconstrained by sense (as in the mad dogs and Englishmen who go out in the noonday sun), fear (like a fighter oblivious to his own safety), or morality. Epitomizing this last usage was Mad Dog Coll, the notorious hit man employed by mobster Dutch Schultz. The mayor of New York bestowed the moniker in 1931 when Coll killed a five-year-old and left several other children wounded during a shootout.

Prairie dog (n) The somewhat dog-resembling desert-dwelling rodent that inhabits the American West. Examples of applying "dog" to other animals that resemble canines in features or traits include "dog-badger," "dog-bat," "dog-faced baboon," "dogfish," and "dog salmon."

Reservoir Dogs (n) The title of Quentin Tarantino's 1992 violent debut film, with no precise meaning to the term. Tarantino insists he intended it as "a mood title" and that people should make up their own definitions. Some of those revolve around the idea of feral dogs that hang around or fall into reservoirs and who attack each other, as do the characters in the movie, which seems as good an interpretation as any.

Salty dog (n) An experienced sailor. **2.** A man with a strong libido. Conjoined in many song lyrics with "candy man," meaning a drug dealer or, more connotatively, a man who provides for a woman in return for sexual favors. "If you can't be my candy man, you can't be my salty dog" sings the Reverend Gary Davis. **3.** A drink made with vodka (or gin) and grapefruit juice.

Sea dog (n) Like "salty dog," an experienced sailor. **2.** A pirate. **3.** The name salty dogs gave to meteors, which they thought foretold bad weather. Other weather-related usages are "water dogs," referring to storm-portending dark clouds moving through the air by themselves, "sundogs," the mock suns or light spots that are sometimes seen on either side of a low-lying sun, and rainbow-like formations that appear in fog. **4.** A harbor seal.

Salty dog

Shaggy-dog story (n) A lengthy joke with unnecessary incidentals in the telling and a generally pointless, anticlimactic conclusion. Also jokes featuring a talking dog, such as: "A religious Jew brings his dog with him to Rosh Hashanah services, insisting to the incredulous offended congregants that the dog can pray, and provoking large wagers that are lost when the pooch stays silent. Later, at home, the dog consoles his angry, bereft owner by saying, 'Wait until Yom Kippur, we'll get ten-to-one odds.'" There are different versions of how the term originated, including one version in which a shaggy dog is entered in a series of contests culminating in a grand finale where the judges declare he's not so shaggy, and another in which someone advertises for a lost shaggy dog and, after many tribulations, the person who answers the ad arrives with the shaggy dog only to be told the missing dog is, "Not as shaggy as that."

Three-dog night (n) A cold night—i.e., one requiring three dogs to keep you warm. Also the American rock group that sang of their friend Jeremiah the bullfrog and wished joy to the world.

Three-dog night

Top dog (n) The person, group, or entity that is in the dominant position, especially when emerging victorious after a conflict. "After twenty years of corporate infighting at Amalgamated Schmaltz, Herb ended up CEO, with all the perquisites that come with being top dog."

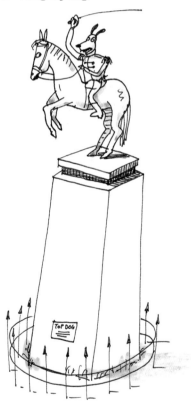

Topdog-underdog (n) The term coined by
Gestalt therapy founder Fritz Perls for the intra-
psychic conflict that people engage in—one part
of their minds (the top dog) demanding that they
behave in a certain way, instructing the individual
with "shoulds" and "oughts" (quit the job, leave the
relationship, lose some weight, clean the house, get
in shape, etc.), while the other part (the underdog)
resists and makes excuses for not complying. Also
the title of the 2002 Pulitzer Prize-winning play by
Suzan Lori Parks about the struggles of everyday
African-American life.

Underdog (n) The person, group, or entity
expected to lose a competition or a political race.
Election night, 1948, Truman was so much the
underdog that the *Chicago Tribune* confidently
headlined Dewey as victor even before the results
were in.

Yaller dog (n) A cowardly person. The demeaning term for a breed of dog indigenous to the Carolinas. In ironic use, the courageous, family-saving, loyal-to-the-death star of the 1957 Disney film of Fred Gipson's children's book, *Old Yeller*.

Yellow dog (n) Back in 1880 it meant someone mean or contemptible, especially someone opposed to trade unionism. By the end of the 19th century it referred to Southern Democrats who, it was said, would vote for a yellow (or, more precisely, "yaller") dog before a Republican.

Yellow dog

A barking dog won't bite

Idioms, Proverbs, and Metaphors

A barking dog won't bite Idiom meaning there's no need to fear the loudly threatening. "Sally said her mother had been promising to divorce her father for thirty-five years, but he was stunned when she served him with papers, figuring a barking dog never bites."

A dog and his bone Stubborn, persistent, relentless. A description of one who hangs on to something protectively, or stays after it without cease. "Josiah had more pressing matters to attend to, but the drubbing Herb had given him over Sally, and his subsequent failure to pursue the relationship, nagged at him until he found his thoughts returning to it and working it over like a dog and his bone."

Barking up the wrong tree Searching in the wrong place for an answer or a solution; to be completely wrong about something, as dogs might continue to pursue prey at a tree from which it has escaped.

Better to be the head of a dog than the tail of a lion A proverb that appears in many forms in many languages, advising that to be the leader of a small or less prestigious entity is better than being subordinate in a large one. A variant is "Better to be first in a village than second in Rome," and, of course, to be a big fish in a small pond.

Bitch (n) A female dog. **2.** For six centuries, a malicious, overly aggressive, or bad-tempered woman, but recently embraced by some feminists and used to connote strong, excelling women. **3.** A slang term of contempt for a subordinate man. **4.** A difficult problem. **5.** (v) To whine or complain excessively.

Bitch in heat (n) A female dog during the approximately three-week period when she is fertile and said to be in estrus and sending out signals to any male dog in the vicinity of her indiscriminate desire to mate. **2.** A woman who behaves in a sexually rapacious manner.

Barking up the wrong tree

Blowing dogs off chains

Blowing dogs off chains A very windy day. "Today it was blowing dogs off chains at ISAF's World Sailing Games" read the headline in *The Daily Sail*, and with winds peaking at 37 knots, races were cancelled for the safety of the sailors and security of equipment.

Bring a dog to heel To gain control over a subordinate who has exceeded his authority. "Bush was either unwilling or unable to bring Secretary Rumsfeld to heel."

Call off the dogs To cease attacking or criticizing someone, or to ease up when inflicting punishment. "When South Carolina's attorney general solicited his conservative counterparts in other states to launch a legal challenge to the newly enacted healthcare legislation, Senator Ben Nelson telephoned to ask him to call off the dogs."

Can't teach an old dog new tricks
The proverb "It is hard to teach an old dog trickes" is found in a 1637 treatise by William Camden, but the idea found expression in different forms at least a century before that. With current awareness of the plasticity of the brain even as we age, and with sixty- and seventy-year-olds regularly taking up new activities and careers, expect this one to be supplanted by "You're never too old to learn."

Cats and dogs Incompatible, naturally hostile. "They didn't take into account the different corporate cultures when they merged, and it was a disaster—they got along like cats and dogs." **2.** Speculative stocks with a dubious history. "Before founding Amalgamated Schmaltz, Herb had graduated from selling fake Rolexes on a street corner to selling cats and dogs for a shady brokerage firm."

Chasing your own tail Wasting one's time, going in circles, making no progress, in imitation of a dog going after its tail. Sports columnist Ron Furlong commented sarcastically on Tiger Woods' failure to finish well in any tournament after six months of trying by claiming, "I tried to find the longest known time for a tiger chasing his own tail in the *Guinness Book of World Records*."

Content as fleas on a dog To be happy in a secure position, with one's needs easily attended to. Interestingly, it's only the cat flea that infects the American dog. After noshing on her first blood meal, Ms. Flea lays up to fifty eggs daily so that in nine months she can produce a trillion descendants—a budget number our content-as-fleas-on-a-dog politicians throw around casually.

Crooked as a dog's hind leg Crooked in both senses of the word—bent and dishonest. "That boundary line he drew was useless, as crooked as a dog's hind leg." "Although Madoff was as crooked as a dog's hind leg, those paid to review and regulate his business—the accounting firms, feeder funds, and SEC officials—were as bad or worse."

Cur (n) A dog or human of no breeding and possessing despicable traits, especially cowardice.

Die like a dog To die debased, without dignity or honor. "In modern war," wrote Hemingway, "there is nothing sweet nor fitting in your dying. You will die like a dog for no good reason."

Dog and pony show (n) A presentation designed to sell an idea or a product, often used dismissively. "In an effort to raise money for Amalgamated Schmaltz, Herb put together a dog and pony show demonstrating the virtues of a single product that could clean dishes and clothes and whiten teeth, and took it on the road to show potential investors."

Dog in the manger Someone who prevents others from enjoying a thing that he doesn't want or for which he has no use. From Aesop's fable about a dog who ferociously keeps cattle from the hay he can't eat but on which he's chosen to lie down. In 1937, Winston Churchill infamously compared the Palestinians to the dog in the manger in rejecting the proposal to allow the creation of a Jewish state by partition.

Even a dog distinguishes between being stumbled over and being kicked Supreme Court Justice Oliver Wendell Holmes invented this proverb when approaching the subject of intentionality in a 1909 lecture on liability under the common law.

Every dog has its day Not Andy Warhol's adage that everyone will be famous for fifteen minutes, but an ancient Greek admonition that the lowliest will have revenge on the most powerful. (The supposed origin lies in the slaying of Euripides by a pack of dogs sicced on him by an enemy.) Shakespeare puts the phrase in Hamlet's mouth: "Let Hercules himself do what he may, / The cat will mew and dog will have his day."

Fit as a butcher's dog A butcher's dog is presumably healthy since he has an abundance of scraps to feed on, although by today's standards he's probably overweight and suffering from high cholesterol.

Go to the dogs "Go to ruin" was the meaning for centuries; then, reflecting the popularity of Greyhound racing in Britain, it came to mean a night at the track, then a bit of fun or adventure. Poet and novelist A.P. Herbert alludes to the practice in his poem "Don't Let's Go to the Dogs Tonight," which title Alexandra Fuller appropriated for her amazing, unvarnished 2001 memoir of growing up in Rhodesia, the child of racist parents in a brutal, violent land.

Hair of the dog (that bit you) A drink to treat a hangover. The notion originated in the belief that the cure to an illness could be found in its cause (persisting today in the homeopathic "law of similars") and specifically in the ancient, non-efficacious practice of treating illnesses stemming from dog bites by placing a hair of the biting dog in the wound.

Have no dog in the fight An expression signifying that the speaker has no stake in the outcome of a dispute.

Hound (n) A dog bred and trained to hunt, most by scent, either on the ground or in the air (Bloodhound or Beagle), some by sight (Greyhound or Afghan). **2.** A person who pursues or chases after things, as in "news hound," "publicity hound," or "autograph hound." **3.** (v) To pursue, chase, or harass.

Hush puppies (n) Originally, scrap food in the form of a basic cornmeal mix to be thrown to the dogs to keep them quiet. Apocryphal sources claim that slaves seeking to escape used them to calm guard dogs, and Confederate soldiers to prevent the other side from detecting them by their barking dogs. Today, mixed with flour and egg, flavored with onion, and fried, they're served in restaurants as a savory side dish. Also, a brand of shoes using a Basset Hound as its emblem.

If you can't run with the big dogs stay on the porch If you can't compete with the best in the field, don't try. Akin to "stay out of the kitchen if you can't take the heat."

In the dog house Temporarily out of favor or in disgrace. "Herb spent two weeks in the dog house after forgetting to keep Albert, Sally's Weimaraner, in the kitchen and he ate all the food she'd prepared for her book club."

Junkyard dog (n) Someone with the vicious attributes of the attack dogs that guard scrap yards from thieves. The phrase was popularized by Jim Croce in his song about Leroy Brown, "the baddest man in the whole damn town / Badder than old King Kong / And meaner than a junkyard dog."

Kick the dog Slang for either feeling bad about something you can't alter, or for doing something insensitive to endanger a relationship. "Sally was so frustrated and helpless to get Herb to control his foul mouth and boorish manners, she came home after a night with him wanting to kick the dog."

Let sleeping dogs lie Don't stir up trouble where none exists. Chaucer is credited with the first use in *Troilus and Criseyde*, in 1380: "It is nought good a slepyng hound to wake."

Lie down with dogs, get up with fleas One cannot escape the consequences of association with the wrong people. The implication is that bad traits of character are as communicable as disease.

Like a blind dog in a meat market Running around blindly, out of control.

Like a dog with a bone An idiom describing someone who hangs on to an idea or a subject, going over it obsessively and refusing to relinquish it, as a dog would guard his bone.

Lie down with dogs, get up with fleas

Live like a dog Living in poor, sad, or inhuman conditions. Similar to "work like a dog," "eat like a dog," "be treated like a dog"—meaning, respectively, to work excessively and for inadequate compensation, to eat poorly, and to be mistreated.

Love me, love my dog A metaphoric way of saying that a person must be accepted along with those people and things close to or attached to her; by extension, to be accepted with one's foibles and weaknesses. Back in the 12th century, St. Bernard (appropriately enough) is claimed to have quoted the proverb in Latin: "*Qui me amat, amet et canem*

meum" (literally, "Who loves me, loves my dog, as well"), although why he did that is unclear. "Sally's friends were disgusted with Herb's drunkenness and discouraged Sally from bringing him around, until she called them on it and declared, 'Love me, love my dog.'"

Man bites dog A journalistic trope signifying that only the out-of-the-ordinary event is newsworthy. "Don't you get it?" cried the cub reporter to his editor, "What could be more 'man bites dog' than this politician who's admitting you can't have services without taxes?"

Mongrel (n) A mixed-breed dog or a human with a multi-ethnic background. It implies inferiority and is always used deprecatingly—most notoriously by the Nazis, and today by racists and supremacists of every stripe.

Mucky pup (n) A messy person, especially a child.

Mutt (n) A dog or human of mixed ancestry. Unlike "mongrel," "mutt" is used currently in a prideful, democratic way, as people have come to appreciate the virtues of multiculturalism and the scientific truth of hybrid vigor.

Not the size of the dog in the fight but the size of the fight in the dog One of Mark Twain's and now America's great aphorisms, suggesting that success is a matter of grit, spunk, determination, and a willingness to persist in the face of obstacles. Twain also observed, "If you pick up a starving dog and make him prosperous, he will not bite you," adding that this was the principal difference between a dog and a man.

One dog barks at something and a hundred dogs bark back This ancient proverb could mean that one man's creative effort flung into the world provokes a multitude of responses, or, more cynically, that the multiplied barks are pointless, empty-headed imitations. A political convention should give you the idea.

*Not the size of the dog in the fight but
the size of the fight in the dog*

Pup tent (n) A portable A-frame shelter made out of a piece of canvas held up by two supporting poles. In the military version, each soldier carries a "shelter half," which button together at the roof line. So-called because it was better suited to a puppy than a person, there are now quality pup tents actually manufactured specifically for camping dogs.

Puppy love (n) Adolescent infatuation, presumed to be evanescent and not deeply felt. Of course Juliet's feelings for Romeo gives the lie to that notion, as do the many long-lived relationships that begin in youth.

Puppy pile (n) A group of entangled people of mixed sexes (suggesting a litter of puppies sleeping or climbing over each other), whose purpose is to cuddle or otherwise express affection.

Put on the dog To behave pretentiously; to dress or behave in a showy manner. "Knowing they were going out with rappers, Herb and Sally decided to put on the dog—showing up in a stretch limo, wearing every bit of bling they could muster, including jewel-encrusted tooth caps and a gold nose bone for Sally."

Running dog (n) A lackey. From the literal translation of the Chinese word that pejoratively describes someone who responds to his master's commands with eagerness. George Orwell argued for the use of precision in political discourse and against the use of this and other such thought-impeding terminology.

See a man about a dog A pretended excuse to leave, especially for a drink or to use the bathroom. "Unable to bear another minute of the conversation, Herb rose and said, 'Excuse me, I have to see a man about a dog,' whereupon he beat a quick path to the bar next door."

Shouldn't happen to a dog An illness or other unfortunate condition of such severity that not even an animal should have to suffer it. The *Oxford English Dictionary* says this is one of the many translated Yiddishisms adopted by non-Yiddish-speaking people.

Sick as a dog Really ill. Referred originally not to illness in general but to stomach upset in particular. Anyone who's observed dogs' willingness to devour anything from socks to grass to carrion—and the regurgitated consequences—knows how sick they get.

Son of a bitch (n) An immoral, mean, or spiteful man. In *King Lear*, Kent addresses Oswald, Goneril's steward, as "nothing but the composition of a knave, beggar, coward, pandar, and the son and heir of a mongrel bitch."

Tail between the legs To be ashamed, beaten physically or metaphorically, and possess the expression or posture of a chastised dog. "At the end of the first debate, the candidate left the stage shaken, his tail between his legs."

Tail wagging the dog A situation in which a minor item comes to dominate the major, or in which attention is fixed on incidental problems to the detriment of more central ones. If the intention is to divert attention from important matters to unimportant ones, the method is to "wag the dog." In the 1997 Barry Levinson film of that name, the electorate is distracted from a White House sex scandal by creating a fictive war. S.J. Perelman once wrote humorously of his escape from the attention of some prostitutes: "It was a case of the tail dogging the wag."

That dog won't hunt An idea that has no merit. The phrase has been in use since at least the 1930s but was popularized when used by Lyndon B. Johnson during his presidency in the 1960s. In 1986 it became lyrics in a Waylon Jennings tune: "Break my heart and then you want a new start / Baby, that dog won't hunt."

The dog ate my homework A transparently ridiculous excuse for failure, especially for not delivering something when it was due.

The dogs bark but the caravan moves on An Arab proverb implying that great forces find their expression despite objectors. A list of such American barking dogs would have to include the arguers against the enactment of Social Security, the isolationists who opposed the United States' entry into World War II, or those who insisted that African Americans, women, and the disabled should not enjoy the same rights as everyone else. There are also, of course, those who railed against modernism in art, music, literature, and anything else that wasn't like what they'd grown up with— and I bet you can think of lots of present-day barkers by yourself.

The scalded dog fears cold water Variously credited as an Italian, Portuguese, and Polish saying, preconditioning by trauma is a reality in any culture.

There's life in the old dog yet An expression of surprise when younger folk discover that people much older than them can do what they can—and sometimes more.

Throw the dog a bone To pacify someone with less than her entitlement, or placate with an essentially valueless gesture.

Throw to the dogs To discard as useless. "Throw physic to the dogs; I'll have none of it," says Macbeth when the doctor admits he has no cure for "that perilous stuff / Which weighs upon the heart."

Tough dog to keep on the porch (n) An impulsive, difficult-to-control person. Hillary Clinton candidly described Bill as a "tough dog to keep on the porch."

Whose dog died? A way of asking why people seem dispirited or dejected. The *Oxford English Dictionary* reports its first use in 1634, in *A Very Woman*, a play by Philip Massinger and John Fletcher: "Whose dog's dead now, / That you observe these vigils?"

Why keep a dog and bark yourself? Don't arrange for a task to be accomplished by another and then do it yourself—that's the message of this ancient proverb, found in a 1583 treatise.

There's life in the old dog yet

Index

You're My Dog, Dawg

Published in 2013 by Welcome Books®
An imprint of Welcome Enterprises, Inc.
6 West 18th Street, New York, NY 10011
(212) 989-3200; Fax (212) 989-3205
www.welcomebooks.com

Publisher: Lena Tabori
President: H. Clark Wakabayashi
Associate Publisher and Editor: Katrina Fried
Designer: J.C. Suarès
Design Assistant: Vince Joy

Cover Design by Vince Joy

Library of Congress Cataloging-in-Publication data: TK

ISBN 978-1-59962-123-4

First Edition
Printed in China

10 9 8 7 6 5 4 3 2 1

About the author and artist

Donald Friedman is the author of the award-winning novel *The Hand Before the Eye* and the internationally praised and translated *The Writer's Brush: Paintings, Drawings, and Sculpture by Writers*. For more information or to contact him, visit his website: donaldfriedman.com.

J.C. Suarès has designed, written, and illustrated more than one hundred books, including *The Hollywood Dictionary*, *Art of the Times*, *Manhattan*, *Dogs in Love*, *Black and White Dogs*, *Hollywood Dogs*, *Fat Cats*, *Cool Mutts*, *Funny Dogs*, and *Funny Babies*. His illustrations have appeared in the *New Yorker*, *Time*, and *Variety*.